Activated Monologues
for Male Characters

ACTIVATED

MONOLOGUES

for Male Characters

edited by Kathryn Funkhouser

Published in 2026 by Stage Partners
PO Box 4795
Stamford, CT 06907
www.yourstagepartners.com

ISBN: 979-8-89099-263-5

Printed in the United States of America

10 9 8 7 6 5 4 3 2 1

Questions? Contact us at info@yourstagepartners.com

CONTENTS

COMEDIC MONOLOGUES

How to Use This Book

"Where's the action?" Any actor approaching a scene asks this question, and we found ourselves asking the same one as we approached the idea of a monologue book. We didn't particularly yearn to publish *The Big Book of People Speaking in Long Paragraphs*. We wanted to create a tool that actors could actively use as they craft a monologue for an audition, class, or performance. The action we aim to take at Stage Partners is always to connect theatre artists with the work of our playwrights—the best resource we can offer. Their plays are filled with great roles to inhabit and characters with surprising things to say. It's up to you to activate them in performance. We hope this book will help get you started along the way.

That's also why we are organizing these volumes by the gender of the characters speaking, rather than the actors that might play them. We're here to offer you the characters the playwrights have crafted, roles to play—and we welcome any actor to explore the roles as written. Note that although all of the characters in this volume *can be* portrayed as male, we've also included some roles that the playwrights have designated as flexible too, so not all of them *need* to be male.

Ready for action? Here's what to look for:

An active verb in bold is included in each monologue's introductory description. How many times have we heard our acting teachers say it? Find the verbs! That's why the introduction to each monologue includes not only an overview of the character and the context of their monologue in the play, but also an active verb. This is a jumping-off point, a place to start in your portrayal—there are always more verbs to find!

● **Meet** prompts provide information about the character written by the playwright elsewhere in the play.

↗ **Play** prompts suggest exercises and ways to play with the portrayal of the character to inform your performance.

⚡ **Note** prompts include casting notes and production notes that are relevant to your monologue.

📖 **Discover** prompts suggest further reading: more plays you can read by the author, more places to find similar monologues, and other resources you can explore to inform your understanding of the monologue.

🔓 **Unlock** prompts are exercises that you can try for any monologue in this book. Trying to crack your monologue, but getting stuck? These are questions to ask yourself to get your character moving, with rules you can adjust to your class or your personal process. There are no right or wrong answers as long as they resonate with you.

READ THE PLAY: Finally, because all of the plays in this book are Stage Partners plays, **every monologue includes access to read the entire play that the monologue is from online for free.** At the end of each monologue, the **READ THE PLAY** section will include information about the play with a QR code and web address for the play's profile page. If you create a free account on the Stage Partners site, you can click the "Read for Free" button on the upper right-hand corner of any play profile page to read the entire script.

Remember, as you work on any monologue, if you find yourself coming up blank, you can always go back to the text and read the full script of the play to find a spark of inspiration.

Now, we've got one last action to give you:

GO!

—Kathryn Funkhouser, Editor

DRAMATIC
MONOLOGUES

THE BOY AT THE EDGE OF EVERYTHING
Finegan Kruckemeyer

When The Boy at the Edge of Everything shares his collection of objects from Earth with Simon, the homesick Earthling who landed on his planet gets upset, claiming the objects as his own since they're from his world. Here, the Boy reveals just how long he's been alone, watching Earth from his roof.

THE BOY

Well sorry but…I have known Earth a lot longer than you.

> *(What he says may be depicted as the two walk up to the roof.)*

I did see it come to be, Simon Ives—one millennia when I was up on the roof. I saw gases and chemicals merge, forces pull things together. There are quite a few planets I've seen turn up, over the years, but this one—it caught my eye. It just looked so…hopeful. It wanted to work. So after that I kept checking in on it, every few centuries.

Soon mountains and valleys formed—water drove its way up through rock, plants drove their way up through water, grew onto land. Forests! They were beautiful. Things began moving, on the surface, things that took on many forms (have you ever seen a *giraffe*? That thing is hilarious). Dinosaurs came along—they were great. Your ones—the beginnings of you—they appeared. And they had hope too!

They started off cold, but they found fire soon enough. The fire melted things into points, the points cut wood, the wood made structures, the structures gave shelter, the shelters held farmers who told the land what to be, held teachers who told the children what they *could* be—they passed on the hope!

And the children became adults…and the hopes became realities! I saw dams and bridges and skyscrapers and airplanes and…these small screens, which…which could *see* you saying hello in one place—and then *show* you saying hello in another! Between people who…who could be way away (on the Edge of Everything, say) and still feel connected. If they wanted to. When they were ready to.

This one little blue and green planet… *(He looks through the binoculars:)* With all those people. All that hope.

    (Beat. He hands the binoculars to Simon.)

And you miss those faraway people, Simon Ives, because you lost them.

But I miss them too… Because we never even got to meet.

🔖 **Meet** The Boy. Per the playwright's note: "He has a universe of things to do, but the silence is absolute—what he craves is communality, and friendships to complement the activities."

📖 **Discover** more monologues in the full script of *The Boy at the Edge of Everything,* as well as Finegan's other plays like *Love* and *Four Found a Mountain.*

READ THE PLAY, a coming-of-age fantasy for 4–30 actors:

yourstagepartners.com/the-boy-at-the-edge-of-everything

In the middle of his overscheduled life, Simon Ives dreams of a place where he can just stop and be. Meanwhile, at the farthest point in the universe, The Boy at the Edge of Everything lives by himself, lonely and bored. When an unlikely fireworks mishap sends Simon rocketing into space, their worlds collide… and neither of them will ever be the same. Deep feeling and joyful silliness sit side-by-side in an adventure for anyone who has ever felt overwhelmed by their days.

THOSE WHO REMAIN TURN THE PAGES
Del Martin

*A vampire-like population is slowly taking over Marcus's hometown. Humans join them through a mysterious Process, which they claim to be voluntary. Marcus and his friends meet in the woods to decide whether it's time to leave while they're still human…or if the situation is really not so bad. Marcus has a strong argument to **persuade** them to go: what happened to his mother.*

MARCUS

I went to wake her this morning. I'm always up before her on Saturdays on account of her having to work a double on Fridays. She usually leaves her bedroom door opened, but this morning it was closed. I…I was gonna knock, but… it didn't seem right, so I just pushed it open and went in. She likes when I wake her and take her order for breakfast. Makes her feel like royalty, she says. I'm the one that cooks on Saturdays so for once she doesn't have to. It's a thing… we enjoy… Or did… *(He stares off for a moment.)* I said, "Get up, Momma." And nothing… So I went to her. Pulled back the covers. Her eyes were closed, she looked almost peaceful. Like maybe she was in the middle of a good dream. But then I touched her arm. She was so cold; I jumped back. I thought, "This is it. She's dead." And then I saw her chest rise. But only a little. Just shallow breaths. I thought she was holding on to life, so I ran to my room to get my phone. I was about to call 911, and I turned around and she was right there in the doorway. She said, "What's wrong, baby?" And I saw her eyes, ice-blue. And she had the mark… You know the one they all get from going through the Process. They have it on their right arm. All in the same spot. Well hers… Hers was on her neck… I stood in my room holding my phone and I just froze. She said, "Come here, baby boy. Let me hold you 'til all your bothers are gone." You know how many times she's said that to me? Any time I was in trouble. Any time I was scared of sometimes. I've heard it all my life... She'd see the worry on me, and she'd take me in her arms and those arms would become my whole world... But this time...when she said it...there was nothing behind it. It was like hearing the recording of a dead person. It's their voice, but you know they're gone. I knew right then my momma was not my momma anymore. And... *(A sigh.)* And that's why she's locked in the upstairs closet right now, and I'm standing here. Now you tell me, that woman who hated those damn vamps more than me, you're saying on her way home past midnight coming from a double shift, she stopped and decided to go get through the Process? Is that what you all are telling me?

📖 **Discover** more monologues in the full script of *Those Who Remain Turn the Pages.* Different members of a community each testify with monologues in a trial that threads together the different parts of this piece.

READ THE PLAY, a thrilling horror-drama for 8–25 actors:

yourstagepartners.com/those-who-remain-turn-the-pages

A group of friends meet in secret about whether it's time to flee their hometown being slowly overtaken by a vampire-like population...unless it's already too late. *Those Who Remain Turn the Pages* is a terrifying and timely triptych of tales that makes life-or-death decisions inescapable for its characters and its audience alike—because when darkness falls, people start to show you who they really are.

This full-length play contains the one-act plays Those Who Remain *and* Turn, *which may be performed as individual one-acts, or as part of the complete full-length.*

YOU'VE REACHED JUSTIN
Christian St. Croix

*Daniel's concerned. His best friend Justin hasn't picked up his phone since they kissed last night…and terrifying creatures seem to be coming from the sky. Daniel leaves Justin a series of voicemails as he crosses town to reach him, learning what is really going on in the apocalypse and within himself. Here, amid the chaos, Daniel **professes** how he really feels.*

DANIEL

Okay…walk…walk, Daniel. I need to…Justin…in case… *(A moment, as he "walks.")* The scar on your arm. You got that when you were eight. You'd grab your skateboard, tie a rope to the back of your big brother's bike and he'd pull you around the neighborhood. One day, he decides to take you down this, like, really steep hill. You were going too fast and you got scared, so you let go of the rope. You scraped your arm up pretty badly. Your brother gave you a nickname. What was it? "Slid." He calls you Slid because you slid across the asphalt. *(A moment.)* You love Charles Bradley. You have all of his albums on vinyl, even the ones that are hard to find. *(A moment.)* You hate avocados. We went to that restaurant in Tijuana, you'd ordered some dish, and it was, like, loaded with sliced avocado. You didn't want to send the plate back, so you picked each of them off, one by one, with the handle of your fork. *(Takes a breath.)* I'm coming, Justin. I'm walking. *(A moment.)* You keep a floor fan in your bedroom. When you were a kid, in Louisiana, your apartment didn't have air conditioning and your mom would run this, like, huge rusty old fan. It didn't do anything but circulate the hot air, but now you can't sleep without the sound. *(A moment.)* You know every single episode of *Buffy the Vampire Slayer* by title, season and episode number. You prefer wine to beer. You're a ride-or-die Steelers fan.

Your favorite movie is *Cat on a Hot Tin Roof* with Elizabeth Taylor. You shaved your head too…when your brother got cancer… *(A moment.)* I've made you laugh. *(A moment.)* Here's what I want you to remember about me: I love you. I love you, Justin. I shouldn't have kissed you without telling you that first. *(A moment, takes a breath.)*

⚡ **Note** the opening stage direction of the play, which specifies that neither Daniel nor Justin holds a phone—"both men speak out to the audience." Also note the playwright's rhythm. Per the playwright: "'A moment' marks short or long dramatic pauses depending on the…moment."

✏ **Play** layers of action. At this point in the play, Justin has learned that the creatures only kill you if you run, so he is also trying to walk calmly down a hallway full of creatures to Justin's apartment. What can you discover in this monologue by adding this second layer of action?

📖 **Discover** additional monologues in *You've Reached Justin*, and throughout the *Ten(ish): Horror* collection.

READ THE PLAY, a 10-minute horror-romance for 2 actors:

yourstagepartners.com/youve-reached-justin

Daniel only planned for a night out of clubbing with his best friend and crush, Justin. But before they can meet, monsters fall from the sky and begin attacking the city. When Justin won't answer his phone, Daniel starts out through the carnage and chaos to rescue him, leaving voicemails along the way. Part sci-fi/horror, part romance, *You've Reached Justin* will keep your heart pounding until the very end.

This play is part of the short play collection Ten(ish): Horror.

ANTIGONE: 3021
Nina Mansfield

*In this futuristic retelling of the classic Greek tragedy
Antigone, Haemon's mother, Creah has taken over as
Chancellor of Thebes, where popular media like the talk
show* The Vista *keeps her in power. But when Haemon's
girlfriend Antigone publicly breaks Creah's unjust law and
Creah sentences her to death to hold onto her authority,
Haemon realizes his mother has gone too far. Here he*
threatens *her with the consequences of her actions.*

HAEMON

When you don't have the support of the people, what kind
of leader can you be?

You'll have to figure that one out on your own. You say you
want to hear what I have to say, but you don't. I question
you—I question you for your own good, and it's like the
tiniest hole poked in your massive ego reveals you're full
of hot air. And when all that air seeps out, what are you
left with? You can't rule without real substance. You can't
rule with the force of your own ego.

I'm not going to be one of those people who just says
what you want to hear. Because you're wrong. Your law
is wrong. The way you've handled this entire situation is
wrong. You can't just kill people who disagree with you.
And I'm not the only one who thinks so. Open your eyes,
mom. Look beyond *The Vista* and look into the actual
streets of our city. I had faith in you once. But now I'm
going to do what I think is right. And don't worry. I'll never
bother you again.

   (Haemon exits.)

✗ **Play** Haemon's arc. From his dialogue in his first scene in the play:

"…I was in the middle of this game. I'm building this world—this totally ideal world—like not just the airways and living pods—but creating decrees—and deciding what gets taught in learning pods. Imagine if we could really do that. Like actually build, from scratch, the world we want to inhabit."

What about his character stays consistent between this point and his monologue? What changes?

📖 **Discover** the full script of *Antigone: 3021*, which includes several powerful monologues.

Antigone: 3021 is a retelling of the classical Greek tragedy by Sophocles. For another version of *Antigone* that takes place during World War II, you can read *Antigone in Munich* by Claudia Haas.

READ THE PLAY, a full-length dystopian drama based on a classic Greek tragedy, for 14–29 actors:

yourstagepartners.com/antigone-3021

It's the year 3021 and Thebes has just been through a bloody civil war. Chancellor Creah has decreed that any-one who buries the body of the traitor Polyneices will face death, but Antigone is determined to bury her brother, no matter the penalty. She brazenly breaks Creah's law and broadcasts her crime on the public cloud. Now Creah must decide if she will bend to the will of the people or punish Antigone for her crime.

A one-act version of this play is also available.

MY BROTHER'S GIFT
Claudia Haas

adapted from the writings of Eva Geiringer Schloss
and the poetry and paintings of Heinz Geiringer

In 1943, the Geiringer family has been in hiding from the Nazis for two years. Teenage Heinz and his father Pappy are now in one location, his mother Mutti and his little sister Eva in another. A talented musician forced to stay quiet in hiding, Heinz teaches himself to paint…and to control his fear.

HEINZ

We moved again. Eva and Mutti also moved. Altogether, we moved seven times. Sometimes our benefactors just got frightened of being caught. Other times, they would blackmail us for more money. After almost two years in hiding, money was running short. I didn't know how much longer this could go on. Painting was no longer a luxury. It was a need—what I needed to survive. We had long since run out of canvas. We painted on any scrap of fabric we could find. We even painted on linoleum!

As the months went on, I stopped painting hope and painted my fears. I had to acknowledge them to cope. I'd lie awake night after night. During the day, I kept myself occupied. But in the dark, the dangers came alive. Would we all survive? I couldn't bear to think of my sister not making it. I wouldn't allow those thoughts. Pappy was always so strong and clever—surely he would survive.

I woke up one morning in a sweat because I had dreamed that it was Mutti who died. Mutti—who was so much a part of me. Mutti who gave me the joys of books and music. The dream was unbearable and the only way I could shake it was to paint it. So I painted a young boy crying while his mother lay dead in the other room. It was as if I painted my fear, I could stop it from happening.

● **Meet** Heinz. Heinz's real-life sister Eva Geiringer Schloss, who shared her writings and memories with the playwright, introduces him in her note:

"He was a remarkable, gifted young boy: a musician, a poet, an artist and a seeker of knowledge. He taught himself five languages while in hiding. I always wanted his short life to be remembered. [...] Through his painting, poetry, and love of languages, he made his time in hiding bearable. I hope he can be a role model for the many young people who are struggling in a very complicated world."

📖 **Discover** resources: Images of Heinz's paintings and drawings can be viewed on the play's page under "Resources," including the one he describes in this monologue. Productions of the play have permission to use them as projections. The playwright provides a list of educational and classroom resources for further reading too, also in the "Resources" section.

READ THE PLAY, a full-length historical drama for 5–15 actors:

yourstagepartners.com/my-brothers-gift

Based on the remarkable true story of Heinz Geiringer—neighbor and friend of Anne Frank—we follow the story of a young artist and loving brother living in unconscionable circumstances. A trained musician at only 15 and now forced to live in hiding and silence, Heinz turns to painting and poetry to express his everyday terror but hope of the future. Through Heinz's inspired paintings, nostalgic love of life, and his sister Eva's remembrances, we are shown the power of art to offer hope and healing.

A one-act version with suggestions for virtual performances is also available.

ELEPHANT/MAN
Del Martin

***freely adapted from* The Elephant Man and Other Reminiscences *by Sir Frederick Treves**

Throughout his life, Joseph Merrick has been exposed to the gaze of others because of his outward appearance, often without his choice in the matter. But here, as his health fades and fantasy and reality blur for him, he chooses to expose what is in his heart to the gaze of the audience— and maybe find an escape through the framework of the play itself.

(Merrick is in bed, sitting up. His head resting on his knees. He is asleep. It's nighttime.
Merrick wakes up.)

MERRICK

Hello?

Oh…

No one.

No one, Joe.

Just the quiet of the night.

> *(Merrick, with some difficulty, gets out of bed. He takes his cane. He crosses to center stage.*
>
> *For a few moments, Merrick stands in silence, looking down at his feet. Eventually, he looks out, at the audience.)*

Good evening, ladies and gentlemen.

Please allow me to introduce myself.

I am Joseph Merrick. Do you recognize the name?

Do you know me?

Or do you simply recall my face?

Some have called me John. And I never bothered to correct them.

I'm grateful to have been in their thoughts.

What is it to be known? Does a name even matter?

To some, I am simply, The Elephant Man.

A name on a poster meant to shock and intrigue.

Is that why you're here tonight?

Do you wish to be horrified?

Or maybe it's not terror that you seek, but comfort.

My mere existence makes people feel better about themselves.

No matter their affliction. No matter their pain. No matter their grief, their sadness, their yearning for something more…

When they see me, in those moments they are made whole. All at once, in my presence, they become something perfect.

Of course, it's only an illusion. But we all get by on dreams, don't we?

(A beat.)

I apologize.

You're not here to listen to me pontificate on the complexities of life.

You want a story.

A tale to take you away.

I, more than most, can understand that.

You want villains…

And friends…

Romance…

And adventure…

You want a hero. But I'm not sure I can give you that.

Don't we always cast ourselves in that role?

And also, I'm tired. I'm so very tired.

(Merrick steps forward, peering out.)

What about you?

(He points.)

Why don't you play The Elephant Man tonight?

Yes, you. Come.

It's really quite simple.

All you have to do is lay down and die.

Come. It will be all right. I promise.

For once, I would like to watch.

◖ **Meet** Merrick: The historical Joseph Merrick was a man with a rare genetic condition that affected his appearance and made speech difficult for him— However, the playwright differentiates how Merrick will be portrayed as a character in this play, noting that performers portraying Merrick should not attempt to recreate his actual appearance in any way, or speak with any impairment—both are conveyed instead by the way other characters react to him.

⚑ **Note** the theatrical convention used throughout the play, per the production notes: When the character of Merrick shares a moment of empathy with another character, the action stops, and the performer portraying Merrick switches roles with the other performer, who steps in to become Merrick. How do the other "switch" moments make this moment meaningful?

- ✐ **Play** Merrick's arc: Each beat within Merrick's monologue echoes something from his memories. What specific characters and lines from earlier in the play might he be recalling in each? What does he achieve as he conjures them up?

- ⤶ **Unlock** monologues by shaking up your rehearsals vocally. Though repetition is key to preparing your piece, you also want to make sure it doesn't start to feel like stale recitation. Stay loose by practicing the monologue in a way you might not ever perform it. Try speaking it at twice the speed that you normally would, then again at half the speed. Try it in a whisper all the way through, then run it again in a bellow. Run it once hitting all the consonants in each word twice as hard as usual, then again, emphasizing the vowels. It's probably going to be a bit silly—and that alone can be great to keep your mind engaged with the words! But you also might notice a new moment in the monologue where a change in volume, speed, or emphasis is exciting and effective, too.

READ THE PLAY, a full-length ensemble-based historical drama for 8–30+ actors:

yourstagepartners.com/elephant-man

The story of Joseph Merrick (a.k.a. The Elephant Man) comes to life in this highly theatrical retelling featuring an ensemble of performers that share the role of Merrick. Whether on a bare stage or with an elaborate set, this adaptable play shines the spotlight on the vivid inner life of Joseph Merrick, and his relationship with the good Dr. Treves. This classic story of the ultimate outcast feels as fresh and as relevant as ever.

TUCK EVERLASTING
Mark Frattaroli

adapted from the novel by Natalie Babbitt

A local girl named Winnie has discovered the Tuck family's secret: a spring hidden in the forest has given them eternal life. Afraid of the secret getting out, but unsure of what to do, they have brought her back to their home. Here, kindly patriarch Angus Tuck takes Winnie out on a rowboat to **warn** *her how disastrous it could be if the secret of the spring becomes known.*

TUCK

But us Tucks, Winnie, we're stuck. Stuck so's we can't move on. We ain't part of the wheel no more. Dropped off, Winnie. Left behind. And everywhere around us, things is moving and growing and changing. You, for instance. A child now, but someday a woman. And after that, moving on to make room for the new children.

…No, not now. Your time's not now. But dying's part of the wheel, right there next to being born. You can't pick out the pieces you like and leave the rest. Being part of the whole thing, that's the blessing. But it's passing us by, us Tucks. Living's heavy work, but off to one side, the way we are, it's useless, too. It don't make sense. If I knowed how to climb back on the wheel, I'd do it in a minute. You can't have living without dying. So you can't call it living what we got. We just *are*, we just *be*, like rocks beside the road. I want to grow again, and change. And if that means I got to move on at the end of it, then I want that, too. Listen, Winnie, it's something you don't find out how you feel about until afterwards. If people knowed about the spring down there in Treegap, they'd all come running like pigs to slops. They'd trample each other trying to get some of that water. That'd be bad enough, but afterwards—can you imagine? All the little ones little forever, all the old ones old forever. Can you picture what that means? Forever? The wheel would keep on going 'round, the water rolling by to the ocean, but the people would've turned into nothing but rocks by the side of the road. 'Cause they wouldn't know till after, and then it'd be too late. Do you see now, child? Do you understand? Oh, Lord, I just got to make you understand!

📖 **Discover** more monologues in the full script of *Tuck Everlasting*. For another great play adaptation of a Natalie Babbitt book by Mark Frattaroli, read *The Search for Delicious* (which is available in both a full-length and a one-act version).

READ THE PLAY, a faithful adaptation of a beloved literary classic for 8–20 actors:

yourstagepartners.com/tuck-everlasting

In 1880, 10-year-old Winnie Foster, trapped by the rules imposed by her strait-laced family, runs away and discovers the humble Tucks who had accidentally stumbled upon a spring long ago that gave them eternal life. Winnie promises to keep their dangerous secret but then a sinister stranger in a yellow suit arrives at their door with intentions to steal the immortal water for himself. Ultimately Winnie must choose whether or not to drink the immortal water and join them in an everlasting adventure—or live on in a natural way, living a life full of the ordinary beauty of growth and change.

LOVE
Finegan Kruckemeyer

Young Oslo got lost in the wind and rain trying to help all of his neighbors in the little town of Mellingong before a big storm. Once he's rescued by his mother, Ruthy, she takes him back to the town hall where all their neighbors are sheltered. Here, he **discovers** *both the wonderful and terrible fallout of the storm.*

OSLO

Everyone's standing outside the town hall, every single person in the whole of Mellingong. And then all of them come up to me and Mum and give us the biggest hugs ever. Tony and Trish cuddle me together, like a cuddle sandwich. And Robert from the pub holds his puppy up so it licks my face. Mrs. Yusgenovitch holds me and won't let go, so I almost get suffocated in her big, old lady bosom. And Mrs. Cho shouts at me like she's angry, and then just shakes her head, and squeezes my cheeks and won't stop rubbing my hair and laughing. And Mr. Trundle sits at the back in a wheelchair and just nods slowly like old people do and says…my dad would've been proud.

And then all of Danica's brothers and sisters jump on me in the back of the milk float. And the last one is Danica—and she doesn't jump on me 'cause… I don't know why, but it'd be weird with her. So I climb out and we just stand there. And it's funny: for the first time ever… Danica can't find the right words.

(*Silence.*)

And it turns out that my love is called: "Just Staring Into Each Other's Eyes for a Long Time, Without Saying Anything" love… And it turns out Danica's is too.

Then I see Danica look behind me, and I do too, and I see… Ah…

(The damage is seen.)

It's unbelievable. Everything's different in Mellingong. Houses are sideways, and some are flatways, and some are just…gone.

- **Discover** more monologues in the full script of *Love,* as well as Finegan's other plays like *The Boy at the Edge of Everything* and *Four Found a Mountain.*

- **Unlock** monologues by finding the shifts and turns. Where *exactly* in the monologue does your character shift? What changes for him physically, vocally, tonally? What exactly incites eachs shift in the moment? Is it something he sees, hears, learns, remembers?

  Try imagining the thing that incites each shift for your character in as much detail as possible. Then, play around with imagining it the opposite to see what you find. For example, if a frightening animal approaches, what if it was beautiful? If someone tells you good news and it was devastating somehow? What changes? Could it be both?

READ THE PLAY, an adventure for 2–15 actors:

yourstagepartners.com/love

Everyone in the little beach town of Mellingong can only take a few important things to their shelter in the big town hall, and young Oslo Rogers wants to help. His fun mother Ruthy is always helping the community, so Oslo goes to each of his eccentric neighbors with an offer to take their "love luggage"—the things they love the most—up to the town hall for them. But he's surprised to hear their remarkable stories of all the different types of love there can be…and how tricky it can be to pack up.

SPOON RIVER
Jason Pizzarello

adapted from The Spoon River Anthology by Edgar Lee Masters

*Each resident of Spoon River has the chance to rise from their grave and share the unfinished business of their lives. After the teacher Emily Sparks speaks of a little boy she helped, Reuben **proclaims** the unrequited love for her that followed him throughout his life.*

(Reuben Pantier now steps forward from his grave. Early 20s, good-looking, charming.)

REUBEN PANTIER

I was Reuben Pantier.

(He looks at EMILY then back out.)

Well, Emily Sparks, your prayers were not wasted,

Your love was not all in vain.

I owe whatever I was in life

To your hope that would not give up on me,

To your love that saw me still as good.

You were the only one.

Oh, Emily.

Let me tell you the story.

I'll skip the part on my father and mother—

Everyone seems to know it.

After that when school was finished...

How do I say this?

The milliner's daughter, Dora, made me trouble.

And so I went out in to the world,

Where I passed through every peril known
Of wine and women and joy of life.
One night, in a room in the Rue de Rivoli,
I was drinking wine with a black-eyed lady,
And suddenly tears swam into my eyes.
She thought they were amorous tears and smiled
For thought of her conquest over me.
But my soul was three thousand miles away,
In the days when you taught me in Spoon River.
And because you couldn't love me from afar,
Nor pray for me, nor write me letters,
The eternal silence of you spoke instead.
And the black-eyed lady took the tears for hers,
As well as the deceiving kisses I gave her.
But somehow
Somehow, in that hour, I had a new vision—
Of you.
Oh, Emily Sparks!

(Reuben, pleased with himself, returns to his grave.)

✍ **Play** Reuben's arc: Before we meet Reuben we hear from a local druggist who speaks of him negatively, followed by Emily Sparks, who speaks of him positively. How does Reuben meet or defy the expectations they set up?

📖 **Discover** Edgar Lee Masters's *Spoon River Anthology,* a classic anthology of poems which was also the inspiration for Thornton Wilder's play *Our Town.*

📖 **Discover** additional monologues throughout *Spoon River,* and read more Jason Pizzarello adaptations of literary works like Guus Kuijer's *The Book of Everything,* Madeleine L'Engle's *The 24 Days Before Christmas,* and Lewis Carroll's *Alice in Wonderland.*

🔓 **Unlock** monologues with objectives. What does your character want when they speak their monologue? Objectives can be big (power) or small (a hamster), physical (food) or a deeper need (validation). Does your character have a single objective or multiple? How can you layer them? For example, if your character's objective is revenge, what if you also gave them the objective to take the ring off their enemy's finger?

Is each objective conscious or unconscious? What does your character think they want, and what do they really want? What happens if you layer a new unconscious objective under your conscious objective? For example, if your character's conscious objective is to steal someone's chapstick, try your monologue once with the unconscious objective to destroy their life, and once with the unconscious objective to marry them one day.

READ THE PLAY, a full-length dramatic adaption of the classic poetry anthology for 8–50 actors:

yourstagepartners.com/spoon-river

Former citizens of a mythical Midwestern town speak from the grave of the day-to-day hopes and dreams of their lives. Touching, anguished, and contemptuous, their voices and stories weave together in this fresh new take on a modern American classic. You won't forget what you've heard from these distinctively small-town folk as they evoke universal themes of hope, despair, and love.

A one-act version of this play is also available.

BETWEEN THE STORIES:
AN APARTMENT PLAY
Laura Neill

*The Super **pressures** the tenants to finish the business they've left undone.*

SUPER

THIS IS NOT YOUR APARTMENT. It was. It WAS your apartment, before you two went on a trip to patch up your marriage and there was a storm and you slid off the road. It WAS your apartment, before you all fell asleep after a long work day and didn't hear the carbon monoxide alarm. It WAS your apartment, before the Alzheimer's took over, before you died of a broken heart. But it's not your apartment anymore. All these noises you hear? You hear them because you're in the same place. The bowlers from the alley that used to be on street level. The farmers who churned butter here, before this was a city. The teenage pots-and-pans band who annoyed everyone in the building before their tour plane went down. And me, the super who got stuck in the basement during the flood that condemned this building. All the layers of this place got thin after it was condemned. It was empty, and the city doesn't like empty spaces, so it drew us out of the ether, all of us with stories we needed to finish. *(To MJ and Pat:)* You needed a morning before work to have a real conversation. *(To Casey and Gab:)* You needed an afternoon to talk about the grandkids. *(To Ash, North, and Len:)* You needed an evening to tell your friends you were moving out. And I needed to fix what was broken, because that's what the super does. But there isn't any time left, because this building isn't condemned anymore. My daughter took out a loan to buy this place in my memory, and she just filled the last apartment. THIS apartment. So your unfinished business? Finish it now. Because there's no space left for us ghosts.

🍴 **Note:** This role is listed as flexible, so the Super may be portrayed as a male character or not, as the actor or production desires. How will you build your character?

✓ **Play** with the plot threads that the Super is weaving together in this monologue to understand the emotional impact of his words. Mark each character or group the Super references in the monologue, then return to the play to find where it is introduced. What expectations are set up for the audience and for the characters themselves in each introduction? How does the Super subvert those expectations here?

READ THE PLAY, a heartfelt one-act dramedy for 10–20+ actors:

yourstagepartners.com/between-the-stories

This apartment building is full of strange noises. Pat thinks it's fun that they might live next door to ghosts, but MJ insists that they just have rude neighbors. North is convinced the ghosts want Ash to come party for birthday month, and Gab thinks the building wants Casey to stop trying to clean out the kids' room. Drew is trying to get Win to ignore the noises so they can move into this cheap apartment… As the noises build, so does the temperature of these conflicts. Stories of love, friendship, and regret collide in close quarters, all to a mysterious (live foley) soundtrack. This heartfelt drama boils over as we get closer to the first of the month—when the lives of everyone in this building will change forever.

THE HAUNTINGS AT CEDAR PARK
Del Martin

As Vern and his friends wait in the park for the others in their group to arrive for an evening of ghost-hunting, they discuss whether they believe in ghosts. Vern does…and here he **confides** *why.*

VERN

I was in Montreal with my folks. This was like four years ago. We were staying in this old hotel. Like my mom picked it because of its charm, but apparently charm just means uncomfortable. And anyway, it was at night. My parents had gone down the street to get Tylenol for my mom. I was in this room by myself. I was watching TV, but it was all in French except for the sports channels they were in English and I remember thinking, I don't know what's worse, *The Big Bang Theory* in French or golf highlights in English. So I turned off the TV. I was just sitting there. In the silence. And then I got up to go to the mini fridge because I had stashed some peanut butter cups, but not the Reese's kind. These were special—from a chocolate shop. Hand-made. So I bend down to the fridge 'cause it's the kind that's low to the ground. I get my peanut butter cups and I'm really excited and then I stand and I freeze.

(Beat.)

I feel it. Right behind me. The hair on the back of my neck stands up. I can barely breathe. And then I feel like I have to turn around. I tell myself, "Look. Just look. Face it." And in my mind, or what do they call it…my mind's eye? In my mind's eye, I could see it, but not really… It was more like I could feel the outline of it. It's there. Right behind me. And then I feel it come closer and I turn around. I don't want to, but I do. And just as I turn around, my parents open the door. And it's gone. Whatever it was. It was there. And then it wasn't. That was our last night there, which was good because I couldn't sleep at all knowing that it was still probably still in the hotel, or in the room… watching me.

(Vern finally looks up at them. The remembered horror still fresh on his face.)

⚡ **Play** with tension: Throughout his story, where does Vern shift between building up tension and releasing it? How might his delivery change in those moments to make them especially effective

📖 **Discover** more monologues by Del Martin on the spooky side. Read the full script of *The Hauntings at Cedar Park*, as well as his plays *In The Forests of the Night* and *Those Who Remain Turn the Pages.*

Can't get enough of all things creepy? Read *Ten(ish): Horror*, which includes several monologues throughout the anthology.

READ THE PLAY, a one-act horror drama for 16 actors:

yourstagepartners.com/the-hauntings-at-cedar-park

Shifting between multiple time periods, we follow two groups of students as they search for a mysterious ghost in blue. They've all heard the legend. And though some don't believe it, for all of the teens who venture into Cedar Park, the legend sure does believe in them. In the end, that's all that matters.

WRECKAGE
Peter Gil-Sheridan

*On the side of the highway, Indiana State Trooper Officer Sims is alone, trying to **report** the indescribable—what he sees from the scene of a terrible crash.*

OFFICER SIMS

Time is all frozen up, backed up behind the wreckage. That's what happens when you're first on the scene. You're witness to reality re-forming itself. It's a quiet process. Doors closing. Lines ending. It won't be long before there's a scab. It'll fall off and the skin will look almost the same as it did before. That's trauma for you…it isn't permanent, it has a death of its own. The action will resume in no time. This one here's pretty bad. Some sort of a shuttle van, a semi—whew! Obliterated. Can't be good inside that van. Bodies lying in the grass. I'll look though…I have to look, it's my job. That's why I do it. I need to see all the jagged edges of experience. You know, the body is a malleable object. Raw material. Clay. Wood. Bronze. And God, well he's quite the sculptor. Anyway, it's never the bodies that get you. It's the stuff: the purses, and the food, and the broken cell phones. The shattered eyeglasses! The glasses have made me…

> *(A shift.)*

All of it is rendered useless in the midst of a highly unexpected decimation.

There will be sounds soon: honking, time is very impatient… and sirens, insensitive, quiet-killing sirens. You have to have them though, that's part of the scene.

I've lived here in Indy all my life. Safest place in the world. And still, people always find a way to die.

- **Note:** This role is flexible, so Officer Sims may be portrayed as a male character or not, as the actor or production desires. How will you build your character?

- **Unlock** monologues with language. What can the type of language that a character uses tell you about them? For example, Officer Sims uses both metaphorical, poetic language (like "the jagged edges of experience"), but also common figures of speech (like "it's the stuff"). What can that tell you about who he is?

  How can you combine other information you find about the character in the text with their use of language? Can it help you make more specific choices? (For example, does this language say something different about a character who works as a police officer, than if the character's profession were a teacher or a doctor?)

- **Discover** more monologues by Peter Gil-Sheridan throughout his play *Wreckage.* For a more comedic Peter Gil-Sheridan play, read *Retreat.*

READ THE PLAY, a one-act ensemble drama for 11–20 actors:

yourstagepartners.com/wreckage

When a van full of young volunteers is hit by a truck, two girls are suddenly connected forever. One holds onto life, wrapped in bandages in the hospital, while the other dies long before her time. Two families struggle, one to hope and the other to grieve. A community of friends, neighbors, and ghosts try to understand. But there is still one truth about the girls that none of them yet knows, and it will bring some of them devastation, and others a miracle in this poetic and powerful ensemble drama.

AND NEITHER HAVE I WINGS TO FLY
Ann Noble

In 1950s Ireland, recently widowed Peter Donnelly has just had dinner with his daughters, Eveline and Kathleen; Kathleen's fiance, Leo Doyle; and Leo's brother, Charlie. Telling stories over drinks after dinner, Peter asks Leo, "Did I ever tell you the story of my lucky rubbish bin?" Here, Peter shares an old family story well-known to his daughters with the newcomers, and also shows them a glimpse into the struggle that makes him who he is, as he **reminisces.**

PETER

Right, as I was saying, it was a frightful night, and I was with my two best friends, Gerry and Pat, and we're hanging about behind this pub, sharing a cigarette. That we found on the ground. Didn't have no money for food, let alone for cigarettes.

...

Gerry was the only one with any money you see, but we'd spent some in the pub that afternoon, and he had a hole in his trouser pocket and he lost the rest. So there we are, starving. Not a thing to eat for two days. I mean, we were coasting on the stout. So, we're having this fag, yelling at Gerry for losing the pound, and all of a sudden we see this dog. He's just trotting by. And we three look at each other and we get this idea to kill this dog and have him for supper.

...

Ay, ay. A mutt like that could keep us for three or four days. So, Pat starts running after this dog, only he has this funny limp you see, because one of his legs was shorter than the other, so he can't keep up with the dog, who by this time, is sensing that he's in great peril. So, Gerry and I start running after Pat, and we pass him in no time. Then this dog runs round this corner and disappears into this pile of rubbish bins. So, Gerry and I are thinking, "There's no way we're jumping into a pile of rubbish for this dog. It's probably got some disease anyway." But then Pat, who's still running to catch up, comes 'round the corner.

And because of his leg, it takes him a long time to get started running, but it takes him an even longer time to slow down. So, he comes flying round this corner and runs straight into Gerry and me, and all three of us fall right into the rubbish. That was the stink of all stinks. And it's not like we could walk into anyone's house and take a bath. So, there we are, sitting in this stink. Now, we're yelling at Pat for smashing us, and he's getting mad at Gerry and me because, "It's not my fault one of my legs is shorter than the other!" So he picks up this rubbish bin and dumps it on Gerry.

No, I saw it coming, so I got out of the way. But hang on for this. This bin he picked up wasn't full of rubbish you see. It was full of sausage and cheese and carrots and bread and all kinds of stuff. Someone must have been hiding it away. So, we start gathering as much as we can. And what else do you think we find?

Don't you! A full pouch of tobacco and cigarette papers.

...

Ay, ay. We figured we'd gone to heaven. There we were eating our full and smoking like kings. And Pat starts walking round like a king. A king that was wounded in battle, you know, his leg and all. "If I were a king," he says. And Gerry starts bowing in front of him saying, "King Pat. Oh, gracious King Pat That Was Wounded In Battle. May I have some of your food?" And all of a sudden...

...

The pound he lost falls out of his shirt pocket and on to the ground. So, we're looking at that pound, and we're looking at Gerry, and we're looking at the sun coming up. And we all three go into the pub for a pint of stout for breakfast! So, for one day, evening to morning, we lived like kings.

Meet Peter: In the playwright's Cast of Characters, she describes him as "a crusty, hotheaded man who loves nothing better than a pint and a good story, especially if he's the one telling it."

Play with the audience. In the context of the play, Peter has four scene partners: two who know the story, and two who are hearing it for the first time. Two are guests, and two are his daughters. How can you make this an asset to delivering the monologue in a solo performance? Could you show greater range if you find moments Peter shifts focus from one character to another? How might Peter's tone or energy shift depending on who he's addressing?

READ THE PLAY, a full-length historical drama for 7 actors:

yourstagepartners.com/and-neither-have-i-wings-to-fly

In this moving family drama set in 1950s Ireland, two sisters' lives diverge as each seeks to forge her own future. When restless Kathleen seeks escape through marriage, Eveline struggles to reconcile her duty to her widowed father with persistent visits from her mother's ghost, who refuses to let her daughter's dreams be pushed aside.

NIGHT OF THE MACABRE
Tracy Wells

adapted from great short stories of Gothic horror. This section adapted from "The Tell-Tale Heart" by Edgar Allan Poe

The wax figures in the museum depicting Edgar Allan Poe's story "The Tell-Tale Heart" have come to life to reenact the tale. So far, the Man has been relaxed with his friend The Old Man, only seeming uncomfortable when his companion takes his eye patch off to sleep. Here, after the Old Man goes to bed, the Man **schemes** *to act on what's been boiling beneath the surface.*

MAN

(Suddenly sinister, talking to himself:)

The eye! Why must he force me to stare at that monstrous orb? A vulture's eye! All day long when it is tucked away behind that dark swatch of cloth I am at peace. I love the old man. He has never wronged me. He has never given me insult. I enjoy his company and his conversation. But once that patch is removed…once that gruesome oculus is revealed…I lose all sense of reason. Calm turns into panic. Thoughts turn to blood. When it falls upon me, my blood runs cold. And so by degrees—very gradually—I made up my mind to take the life of the old man, and thus rid myself of the eye forever.

(Shakes his head.) I'm not mad…no, not even a little. Madmen are impulsive. Madmen can't think logically.

But I am nothing if not cautious and sensible. I have never been kinder to the old man then I have this week. All day long I would sit with him and eat with him and keep him company.

A better friend than I he has never known.

(Sinisterly, creeping slowly closer to the bedroom:)

But at night...as the clock struck midnight...I crept to his room and turned the latch of his door and opened it—oh, so gently! And then, when I had made an opening sufficient for my head, I put in a dark lantern, all closed, closed, that no light shone out, and then I thrust in my head. *(Laughs sinisterly.)* Oh, how cunningly I thrust it in! I moved it slowly—very, very slowly, so that I might not disturb the old man's sleep. It took me an hour to place my whole head within the opening so far that I could see him as he lay upon his bed. Ha!—would a madman have been so wise as this? And then, when my head was well in the room, I undid the lantern cautiously—oh, so cautiously—cautiously I undid it just so much that a single thin ray fell upon the vulture eye. And this I did for seven long nights—every night just at midnight—but I found the eye always closed; and so it was impossible to do the work; for it was not the old man who vexed me, but his Evil Eye. And every morning, when the day broke, I went boldly into the chamber, and spoke courageously to him, calling him by name in a hearty tone, and inquiring how he has passed the night. He would have been a very profound old man, indeed, to suspect that every night, just at twelve, I looked in upon him while he slept.

(Creeping closer:)

But tonight is the night. I can feel it. Tonight is the night I put the eye to rest...once and for all!

⌛ **Discover** the full script for more great monologues from Tracy Wells based on classic horror stories, such as "The Red Room" and "The Yellow Wallpaper." For more Tracy Wells adaptations of classics, read her take on Greek myths, *Myth-Guided.*

READ THE PLAY, a comedic horror anthology for 11–36 actors:

yourstagepartners.com/night-of-the-macabre

A hunt for horror finds four friends at the Museum of the Macabre…a wax museum displaying scenes from short stories by great authors of Gothic Horror like Poe, Hawthorne, and Irving. But as unnerving as the exhibits—and the stories behind them—are…the real terror for the fearless four comes when the exhibits start to come to life! This easy-to-stage play celebrates great short stories of Gothic Horror, including:

"The Birthmark" by Nathaniel Hawthorne
"The Hand" by Guy De Maupassant
"The Monkey's Paw" by W. W. Jacobs
"The Tell-Tale Heart" by Edgar Allan Poe
"The Red Room" by H. G. Wells
"The Velvet Ribbon" by Washington Irving
"The Yellow Wallpaper" by Charlotte Perkins Gilman
"The Shadows on the Wall" by Mary E. Wilkins Freeman

Perfect for Halloween, one-act competitions, or working in collaboration with English Lit teachers, this flexible, large-cast play will delight audiences and actors alike.

Length note: Any of the short stories may be cut to create a shorter play.

FOUR FOUND A MOUNTAIN
Finegan Kruckemeyer

Brian and his older sister Lily are on a quest, trying to save the crumbling town where they've moved after their parents split up. Here, all seems lost when a sudden storm traps them in a mountain cave with their friends Mickey and Arlo and the skeleton of a long-lost explorer—but when the other three succumb to the cold and fall asleep, Brian **inspires** *himself to take charge.*

BRIAN

And that's where we'd have ended. And a long time later (in another hundred years maybe) people would have found four more skeletons, beside old Cressy's one. Because all the people who were good at saving the day, they'd given up.

(Looks at Mickey:) Those ones who can invent things.

(At Lily:) Or inspire people.

(At Arlo:) Or who can make you laugh and keep going even when you want to stop.

Those ones had run out of ideas, and inspiration, and laughter. So that the only one left was the one who usually went along with the rest. That one kid who has ideas too, and is inspired too, and makes jokes too…only in a quieter way. *(Watches Lily:)* That kid who feels sad about his mom and dad too—even if he decides not to share that with anyone. Even if his way of thinking about that stuff is to just do it quietly, just by himself.

What happens when that kid, who usually goes along with the rest, suddenly has no rest to go along with?

> *(He makes a decision and moves to all, waking them.)*

Guys. I've decided.

✎ **Play** Brian's arc: As Brian indicates each of the other characters in this monologue, find the specific moments in the play he might be referring to when he describes each of their gifts and how he follows their lead. How is it different for each? What does it mean to him to flip around each dynamic in this moment?

📖 **Discover** more monologues for male actors in the full script of *Four Found a Mountain*, as well as Finegan's plays *Love* and *The Boy at the Edge of Everything*.

READ THE PLAY, an adventure for 4–11 actors:

yourstagepartners.com/four-found-a-mountain

When Lily and Brian's father moves their family of three back to the cozy little town where he grew up, they are surprised to find it quite different than he remembers. As times have gotten harder, the town itself and the connections between the people who live there have both fallen into disrepair. Yet there are new connections to make, and when Lily and Brian join forces with two new friends to find out the truth about a second moon that appears in the sky, a mysterious code, and a missing explorer, maybe there's hope for the future. An adventure for all ages about the power of young people to remind their community of what it once was and what it might become.

IN THE FORESTS OF THE NIGHT
Del Martin

*Forced to play a mysterious game in the forest at night outside the boarding school all the players attend, the player known only as Two has stepped forward in the place of player One to be the one to tie player Thirteen to a tree to await an unknown fate. When Thirteen asks why, Two **confesses** the sin he's atoning for by taking on this terrible task.*

TWO

On the first day of school, One was in the hallway, by himself, he looked so small. And, this kid came along, this big kid. I think his name is Carlyle. You know him. Real smart and real dumb all at once. Anyway, this kid, this Carlyle, he just knocks One's bag out of his hands and onto the floor and continues on his way. Didn't stop and say anything. Barely even looked at One. But he saw someone small in his periphery and he did what he must have done a thousand times in a thousand ways before…he became destruction. And then he was gone. And left there in his wake, was One, crying and shaking. And me, watching and silent. When something like that happens, so random and broken, my instinct is to run. Run for something more sane. Something I can wrap my head around. I said nothing to One. I left him there, crying. I don't think he knew that I saw, but still… I have the same dreams as everyone else, obviously. But I also have one that is my own. One, in the hallway, crying and shaking and me trying to run away, but unable to move my legs. Stuck with that boy's sadness. His name is Richard. He's a nice boy. I wanted to help him for once.

Note: This role is listed as flexible, so Two may be portrayed as a male character or not, as the actor or production desires. How will you build your character?

Discover more monologues by Del Martin in plays like *Elephant/Man, Those Who Remain Turn the Pages,* and *The Hauntings at Cedar Park.*

Unlock monologues by asking: Who is your character talking to?

If it's another character in the play, at what point are the two characters in their relationship? What history do they have? Does the relationship change over the course of the monologue?

If they are addressing the audience, what does the audience mean to them? What do they want from the audience? How do they hope or fear the audience will react? Does the relationship change over the course of the monologue?

READ THE PLAY, a thrilling one-act drama for 13 actors:

yourstagepartners.com/in-the-forests-of-the-night-by-del-martin

Thirteen students are compelled by their dreams to play a game in the woods to keep a mysterious monster at bay. Not everyone gets to play it again.

#CENSORED
Maria McConville

*When a controversial painting (the content of which is unknown to the audience) is displayed in a school, the community is divided about what to do—but Sam is divided in his own mind. Here Sam **debates** where he stands.*

SAM

Truthfully?

I liked the painting. I think it shows a lot of talent.

I think it's evocative.

Adjective.

Bringing strong images or symbols to mind. Powerful.

I mean…so that part's good.

And I think I believe it's important to be able to you know, speak your mind.

Or paint your mind…I guess in this case.

My issue is just that— this isn't a museum.

Or even a public space really.

We are FORCED to come here.

You can't just look away or stay home.

Everyone should feel comfortable.

And even though it didn't bother me—it did bother a LOT of people.

To see.

THAT.

And no one has a choice to come to school. So, I think.

I mean, I guess that means it's not fair to force your opinion on people.

In a place they are FORCED to come.

Right?

Isn't that the same as separation of church and state?

This is why we're not supposed to pray in school, too.

Because everyone thinks different stuff about that.

On the other hand. Maybe it's good to be exposed to different kinds of thinking?

And like I said it is a good painting…

So I guess.

If they just make sure to put up warning signs?

Then it's ok?

Or maybe not.

(Sighs, exasperated.)

Gosh, it's so hard to tell.

What's the difference between freedom and oppression?

When does my freedom oppress you?

And when does your allegedly oppression like, oppress my freedom?

Where's the line?

…And who decides?

- **Meet** Sam, introduced in the Cast of Characters as "Your average high schooler—probably takes honors classes."

- **Note:** This role is listed as flexible, so Sam may be portrayed as a male character or not, as the actor or production desires. How will you build your character?

- **Discover** monologues for many of the other characters in *#Censored* who have opinions of their own about the painting. For another Maria McConville play filled with great monologues from different perspectives, read her drama, *#Viral*.

READ THE PLAY, a one-act drama for 7–30 actors:

yourstagepartners.com/censored

In this ensemble-driven drama, a school art fair becomes embroiled in controversy when a student unveils a divisive painting. Students, parents, and teachers must ask themselves tough questions about freedom of speech, appropriateness, what art is supposed to do, and "what is the cost of censorship?" 

COMEDIC MONOLOGUES

LAST DAY OF SCHOOL
Ian McWethy

In the hallway on the very last day of school of senior year, nervous Dave announces to his best friend Brian that he intends to ask out his crush…and promptly chickens out. When Brian barely looks up from his phone during this process, Dave accuses him of not having his back. Here, Brian finally snaps and **admonishes** *his best friend.*

BRIAN

I'm just…I guess I'm just having a hard time Dave. A hard time understanding why you can't understand why I might be a bit skeptical about you, Dave McDonald, asking out Madison Montgomery out on a date. Can you not think of why I might be a tad bit cautious? Hm? Can you really not? …Dave… I have been listening to you talk about Madison for four years now. Four years Dave! And throughout those four years I supported you. I did. I supported you when, as a freshman, you told me your locker was next to the most beautiful girl you'd ever seen and that you wanted to ask her out and that nothing was gonna stop you! Well nothing did stop you but guess what?! You didn't ask her out! And then sophomore year, when you said you were going to ask Madison to homecoming, because it was your destiny! Your destiny you said! But did you ask her out then? No. You didn't. Because you swore that you were coming down with mono! Not that you had any symptoms of mono. No, as far as I could tell the only thing you had was a weird rash on your armpit. How is an armpit rash mononucleosis! How do you confuse the two! They're not anything alike Dave! You clearly just chickened out!

(Brian takes a deep breath.)

Look the point is, it seems like every six months you have some sort of epiphany about how now is the "right time" to ask Madison out. And then every time you go to ask her out, you get scared and make up some excuse. You have piano practice or she's a Gemini or you heard a weird rumor that she "will never date anyone while she's in high school and will only date twenty-year-olds." And now you're telling me that this time…this time you're actually gonna do it. This time it's different?! Is that what you're telling me?! I just can't listen to you do this again! Okay! So! Dave! Yes, I am being a good friend by sitting here and not encouraging you. Because I have two options. I can listen and keep my mouth shut. Or I can take all my frustrated anger and disappointment over the past four years and…just…grab you and shake you until you grow a backbone!

↗ **Play** with some improv to find how Brian's frustration reaches a boiling point here. What other tactics might he have tried during Dave's previous attempts?

READ THE PLAY, a full-length dramedy for 4–18 actors:

yourstagepartners.com/last-day-of-school

On the final day of classes at Rochester High School, a renegade student takes over the morning announcements and proposes that everyone do something bold. Or unexpected. Or brave. Or stupid. The point is, you may not have another chance, so now's the time to stop being a wallflower and kiss the girl (or guy!). To let your enemies know that you have always hated their guts. Or to do something as simple as climb the rope in gym without throwing up. Through a series of interconnected scenes, misconceptions, grudges, and secret crushes come out into the open in hilarious and surprisingly touching ways.

A one-act version of this play is also available.

HATERS
Don Zolidis

Wilson High School has been issued a recycling challenge by a pop superstar, and Tommie **boasts** *to the audience there's no limit to what he is willing to do to get enough cans to win the promised concert...in a way that's more disturbing than impressive.*

TOMMIE

So I went over to my grandma's house 'cause I figured she might have a lot of cans to recycle? Nothing. She had no cans. But she did have money in her wallet because she's an old person and she carries cash. So that was awesome, because she also takes a lot of naps, so I just waited for her to fall asleep. Costco has a special on cases of Kirkland cola, which is like, really really terrible right, so no one wants it and it's cheap? For a hundred and twenty dollars you can buy sixteen cases of thirty cans each. I tried to drink one of them and it was like drinking sadness, so I just poured them all out in my yard, to feed the grass. The grass died or whatever but I figure it's a small price to pay to save the planet.

Check it out: Four hundred and eighty cans! Woo.

My grandma is pretty sure she got robbed, though. So she's kinda scared these days and isn't sleeping but um...there are trade-offs.

She might have more cash tomorrow though.

🕯 **Note:** This role is listed as flexible, so Tommie may be portrayed as a male character or not, as the actor or production desires. How will you build your character?

- ✎ **Discover** many monologues for male characters by the prolific Don Zolidis in plays like *The Seven Torments of Amy and Craig* and *The Littlefield Gazette Does Not End Today.*

- ⌙ **Unlock** monologues: If you're struggling to connect physical action to your character, try an unconnected one! Play around with simple actions that *don't* apply to the monologue or the play at all. How would your character deliver this monologue while making a sandwich? Exercising? Building with Legos? Maybe your character is a king who would never make himself a sandwich, but you might find he'd assemble one with perfect efficiency, and think of ways to show efficiency in the way he moves his hand or takes a step. Need to get out of your head? Put different actions into an online randomizer, or on scraps of paper you can pick out of a hat to try as you speak. If you're in a group, have a scene partner come up with an action to challenge you.

READ THE PLAY, a one-act comedy, 15–30+ actors:

yourstagepartners.com/haters

The recycling program at Wilson High School is garbage, until megastar Taylor Swift issues them a challenge: if they recycle 20,000 cans in two weeks, she'll sing at their dance. The whole school leaps into delirious action, cancelling classes to scour the side of the highway, raid recycling bins, and down cans of Monster like water. It looks like they just might make it…which is unfortunate for Naia, who created the deepfake Taylor video challenge for her own scheming ends. Looks like "Taylor" is going to have to up the ante on her challenge. But what will Naia do when the school of desperate Swifties turns to actual crime to meet her demands? Find out in the wickedly funny *Haters.*

WHEN JACK MET JILL
Adam Szymkowicz

*Surprisingly, Jack is in jail. Here, he mockingly **rehashes** how he got into this absurd situation as though he's receiving an award.*

JACK

Thank you for coming. It's been a whirlwind. Truly an honor. People ask me. They say, "Jack, how do you do it?" Well, today, I'm here to tell you all my secrets. I don't want to say it's easy to be me and to do all the things I've done. But with practice and persistence, you too can accomplish what I managed to accomplish in a few simple steps. But you have to believe in yourself. And you have to trust your worst instincts.

How to find yourself in jail, Part 1: The Awakening. First maybe there is something in your life that you know you shouldn't do. This is maybe something you also really want to do. It might be physical violence or illegal drugs. It might be grand theft auto or bank robbery. Or maybe it's stealing gnomes from people's yards. So the first thing is that even though you know you shouldn't do this, you do this thing. And then you do it again. And again. And again. Until you have like a lot of gnomes. Like a whole lot. Like someone might come over and see them and go, "Why do you have so many gnomes? What can someone even do with that many gnomes? Why would you do this?"

And maybe there's no easy answer. Except you know, the normal ones. Bad childhood. Hole inside you nothing will fill.

And then one day, you're a little sloppy and someone sees you and recognizes you and then the cops are there asking questions. And you answer the questions truthfully because at the end of the day, you just want it to be over and as they say, light is the best disinfectant. I also like white vinegar because it's non-toxic and I don't mind the smell. So the cops are there with their guns and their badges and their serious faces and they ask you point blank. So you bring them out to the shed and they say, "Holy shit," and then they take you for a ride. And that's why I'm here. So. That. Is. How.

But you may ask, "What next?" "What are your future plans now that this exciting project has come to an end?" and I have to admit, I don't really know. I never thought that far. It's a relief and also, you know of course I don't feel any better, at all. So… So… So. So. Sob.

- ✎ **Play** with the other pivotal moments Jack processes in the play. How do his tactics this moment compare? Is there anything you can bring to this scene from those moments, or does this one contrast?

- 📖 **Discover** Adam Szymkowicz's monologues, which are beloved by many actors—and you can find more great ones for male characters in his plays like *Heart of Snow* and *The Girl Who Cannot Be Hurt.*

READ THE PLAY, a one-act relationship dramedy for 4–20+ actors:

yourstagepartners.com/when-jack-met-jill

You never know what moments will be pivotal. An existential crisis, or a change in your soda-drinking habits. An unfathomable loss, or a moment of uncertainty about whether you're looking at a possum or not. For Jack and Jill, it's all of the above, as moments across time (and sometimes, between realities) converge into a poignant collage rendering of their relationship.

WHEN BAD THINGS HAPPEN
TO GOOD ACTORS
Ian McWethy and Jason Pizzarello

At the beginning of this production of The Wizard of Oz, *Dewey has forgotten his monologue…but nobody is able to give him a line, so he's sent back out onstage with instructions to simply talk to the audience for two minutes. Now, Dewey tries to* **improvise** *what to say.*

DEWEY

Hi my name is Dewey. I'm playing a character named Farmer Ben. And we're doing *The Wizard of Oz*. Oh, also we're doing a one-act version so that we could do it in competition and our teacher adapted it herself but…it's kind of a mess. I'm not sure this shortened version makes a lot of sense and like…we never really got through tech and our director wasn't really around that much so…yeah. I think this is a mess. I mean, for pete's sake, I'm playing Farmer Ben. The nephew of Dorothy. Who is that?! He's not in the movie. Or the book. He's just a character our teacher made up to make it easier to follow but… I think if anything it's more confusing. Especially since I can't remember my lines and I'm just blabbing on and on. Oh and I have to do this again at the end of the play. Which, you know, I swear I'll memorize the last monologue. I'll have the whole play to sit back and make sure it's memorized but uh…for now…sorry. I got nothin'.

(*Beat. Dewey waits.*)

Has it been two minutes? Anyone? Um… *(Getting extremely awkward now.)* I don't know what else to talk about. Does anyone watch *Game of Thrones*? I'm not allowed to watch it but I got my cousin's password to HBO Go so I've been watching it. It's awesome. I mean some of it's really gross. But overall it's awesome. I like dragons. Hmmm…

(Dewey looks around the stage.)

Waka-waka. *(Beat.)* That's uh…Fozzy Bear. From *The Muppets*. I don't know why I did that. Yep. So… I'm gonna leave now. Hope you enjoy our one-act version of *The Wizard of Oz*. I'm sorry I forgot my monologue.

(Dewey walks offstage, almost proud of himself for getting through it.)

Discover more great comedies cowritten by Jason Pizzarello and Ian McWethy together, such as *The Day the Internet Died* (one-act and full-length versions) and *All The Ways the World Will End (But Not You)*.

For more comedic monologues by Ian McWethy in this book, check out Brian's monologue from *Last Day of School* and Coach's monologue from *Win or Lose*. For more by Jason Pizzarello, look at Phil's monologue from *The Cast List* and Jack's monologue from *101 Breakups*.

READ THE PLAY, a one-act backstage comedy for 10–30 actors:

yourstagepartners.com/when-bad-things-happen-to-good-actors

A simple one-act production of *The Wizard of Oz* gets derailed by missed cues, forgotten lines, and a renegade sound board op who refuses to play anything but dinosaur noises. A comedy that proves, when it comes to live theatre, everything that can go wrong, will go wrong, and it will be hilarious.

THE CURIOUS CASE OF THE COTTINGLEY FAIRIES
Claire Wittman

*In the midst of World War I, a young girl's photographs that appear to show fairies have become a news sensation. Here, the famous author and supernatural enthusiast Sir Arthur Conan Doyle, calls to **provoke** his very best frenemy to investigate with him: the magician and supernatural skeptic, Harry Houdini.*

DOYLE

Harry! Hullo—hullo—can you—ah, there you are, Harry! How's Bess?

Good, jolly good. And you? Quite recovered from being buried alive? Too soon to joke about it?

Well, if I can dig up Sherlock Holmes, surely you can dig up yourself.

What do you mean, "it's different"? It's not diff—well, never mind, then. Are you going to try again?

I'll believe *that* when I see it.

Listen, have you heard about this Cottingley fairy business? Two girls have photographed what they present as living, breathing spiritual creatures.

I'm looking at them now. Have you go the London Standard, morning or evening?

Well, have someone fetch a copy, as soon as you may.

Harry, I believe there's something to it. They've had dozens of locals out…reporters and reverends and the Theosophists, and a fellow from Kodak to verify that it wasn't something the matter with the cameras.

Yes, I know one man's opinion isn't conclusive. That's why

I'm going to see for myself. You ought to come, too—can you get away?

I understand. Those milk cans won't escape themselves, after all. But you ought to be involved— who do you trust to come as proxy?

Frank Canfield? Terrible tabloid nuisance, isn't he? Not exactly a high mark of your faith.

I'm bringing along Madam—no, don't start with me. Don't look at me that way. Yes, I can tell how you're looking through the telephone! I'm bringing Madam Spinoza, no matter what you or Jean or anyone else has to say about it. Marvelous old woman. Told me things about myself I didn't even know! So send your skeptical reporter. Send anyone you want. I know what I think.

"When you have eliminated the impossible, whatever remains—*however improbable*—must be the truth."

Yes, I'm quoting myself, and what of it?

Well, then. Goodnight, old chap—ah, hold now, I'll cable you the girls' address for Canfield! Goodnight, Houdini.

📖 **Discover** the inspiration behind this play, the fascinating true story of the Cottingley Fairy photographs, which even involved Sir Arthur Conan Doyle and Houdini. What can your research about these historical figures and the photos bring to your performance?

For another historical piece that explores the world of Arthur Conan Doyle, read Claire Wittman's play *Moriarty's Daughters*.

↜ **Unlock** monologues with tactics: What different means does your character use to try and achive their objective? How do they try to get what they want?

Where exactly in the monologue does your character shift from one tactic to another? Why does your character shift tactics when they do? Do they encounter an obstacle? Does another character push back? Do they lose their nerve?

As an exercise, try placing an object across the room from you or have a scene partner stand in for your objective. As you read the monologue and move across the room toward your objective, try to physically move in a different way every time you switch tactics in the monologue. For example, if your scene partner across the room has a dollar, and the dollar is your objective, and your first tactic is to intimidate them, you might at first move threateningly...then, if you shift to giving them a compliment, you might start dancing toward them charmingly. See what you can discover about creative ways to portray your character's tactics.

READ THE PLAY, a historical fantasy for 14–21+ actors:

yourstagepartners.com/the-curious-case-of-the-cottingley-fairies

When Lilli Barnes was sixteen years old, she saw a fairy. Encouraged by her impressionable little cousin Mabel, Lilli snaps a photograph, and suddenly, what started as a magical game to distract from the worry of the Great War becomes a national sensation, attracting gullible authors, skeptical reporters, and eccentric spiritualists from all over the world. But swept up in the strangeness of their supernatural sighting, and daunted by the pressures of newfound fame, Lilli and Mabel are left to wonder if they can believe their eyes...or if the "magic they've uncovered is merely imagination gone wild.

SINK! A TITANIC MURDER MYSTERY
Briandaniel Oglesby

*On a film set in the 1990s, the tyrannical director Scott Moody demands that his cast do a dangerous stunt—and when they threaten to quit, he **bullies** them back in line.*

SCOTT

You know what happens when you quit Scott Moody? He puts you on The List. And then he calls your parents out in Nowheresville, Ohio. He says, Moms, Pops, it's your kid's boss. He's about to live in his car. So put Grandma's homemade comforter on his childhood bed, and give him a call, tell him Dad's cough is getting worse and Mom's arthritis is making the chicken-killing too hard, and you really want him home to take over the family puppy mill and marry the toothless neighbor girl—because your child is a Hollywood failure. You want that?

That includes you, Brook. So while they set up, I'm going to be in my trailer watching *The Pirate's Wife* and eating queso. We're back in one hour. If you're not at Lot B, you better be on an airplane to Ohio.

We're gonna make this a night to remember.

- **Meet** Scott: the playwright introduces Scott in the Cast of Characters as an "angry, petulant, dangerous director willing to sacrifice actors for his art."

- **Play** with range within your action to find different levels to play. For example, if you are playing bullying by moving aggressively, is there a moment your character might be especially scary by choosing to stand perfectly still? If your character is a fast talker, could he start slowly and work his way up to speaking with incredible speed? If your character is a yeller, is there a moment he suddenly whispers? Find moments of surprise!

- **Read** the full script of *Sink! A Titanic Murder Mystery* to discover how deep the many layers of this play can go. For more plays by Briandaniel Oglesby, read *The Twelve Huntsmen* and *The Odyssey: A Comedy (Until It's Not)*.

READ THE PLAY, a full-length mystery-comedy for 12–24 actors:

yourstagepartners.com/sink-a-titanic-murder-mystery

Isn't the Titanic the perfect setting for a murder mystery? The glamorous passengers, the conveniently distracting iceberg, it's all fun and games for Detective Tennessee Blossom…until the captain announces that nobody in the first-class lounge can board a lifeboat until they discover the murderer among them. But then, who are these people and what is this place, really? Are we even in a classic Edwardian mystery, or sinking into another genre altogether? Each of the nesting layers of this puzzle-box holds a surprise in this mind-bending, hilarious mystery-comedy.

THE CAST LIST
Jason Pizzarello and Rocco Natale

The cast list has finally been posted for the school play, and Jeremy is trying to decide whether to initial next to his name to accept his role. Phil, a basketball player who also does theatre, **instructs** *him to have a little perspective.*

PHIL

I played basketball since I was three. My dad played. My brothers played. So I played. The thing is… I've been terrible at basketball since I was three. I mean: terrible. I think in all the years since three I've made five baskets and (at least) four of those were accidental…the fifth was for the other team. So when I broke my foot in September I thought, maybe I'll try something new. And honestly… I guess if I'm being honest I didn't enjoy basketball that much. It's a unique hell to be committed to something that you're terrible at AND don't enjoy. Anyway…

My friend Chantal tried to convince me to do the play last year, and I didn't. So she was in the play and I wasn't. Then I saw the play and it was great, so I kind of regretted not doing the play—especially because I'm so bad at basketball. Tryouts and auditions are usually at the same time. But this year I had a good excuse to audition. So I auditioned.

I don't really understand the cast list. I mean I understand the cast list, but I don't understand why everyone gets upset about it. I come from sports, which means that everyone's on the team. Sure you may get more playtime if you're good, but everyone is better than me at basketball, so I was used to sitting on the bench. I guess my point is I didn't care what I was on the cast list of a long as I was on the cast list.

When the list was posted there was all this talk about who got what and who was robbed. Really, it all went over my head. I don't know who deserved to get what parts.

I just assume that it's a good cast list. I'm happy to be on it. Honestly, the more I think about it these actors need to think more like a basketball team. You can't win without passing the ball, and that's I guess like knowing your lines. Someone has to be able to shoot and score, and you need to know where you're going. But mostly if you're on the team you're on the team. So I guess…just be on the team. I'm pretty happy to be at practices… I mean rehearsals. I have to get used to that. Rehearsals. I just wish everyone else was just happy to be on the team.

(Phil dribbles off.)

📖 **Discover** more monologues in the full script of *The Cast List*. For more backstage comedies by Jason Pizzarello, read *This Murder Was Staged, Places in Five,* and *When Bad Things Happen to Good Actors.*

READ THE PLAY, a one-act comedy for 10–30 actors:

yourstagepartners.com/ the-cast-list

Ah, the cast list. Oh, the drama. The casting would be simple if it weren't for constant script cuts, actor trade agreements, backstabbing, helicopter parents, hysterical prima donnas, and the Assistant Director could figure out how to incorporate the songs of *Grease* into *Romeo and Juliet* without getting sued. This is a show for any student who has ever been cast or miscast in a school play or any teacher who has ever attempted to post a list without serious backlash.

THE SEMI-AMAZING, SORT-OF SENSATIONAL, ALMOST UNBELIEVABLE CHRISTMAS SPECTACULAR!
Jon Jory

After both the cast and the audience have agreed that nobody wants to go on with a production of A Christmas Carol *as part of their school's Christmas Spectacular, the actor who is supposed to play Jacob Marley rushes onstage wrapped in his character's trademark ghostly chains to* **protest**.

MARLEY

Are you crazy? I was turkey-boy for two years and now I'm Jacob Marley! Do you know how long it takes to get into these chains and wear this smelly costume? "I wear the chains I forged in life!" I am a thespian! A thespian to the core! Do you know how I get into the mood for this part? I have Mary Ann Belcher slap me over and over backstage—over and over and over! Do you know how Mary Ann prepares to slap me? All summer she soaks her hands in brine—which to the uninformed is pickle juice and salted water—which hardens her hands until they are like cement and then she slaps me and slaps me and these chains are heavy and leave big welts on my wrists and ankles, and the smell of the costume makes me nauseous and I begin to hyperventilate and Mary Ann Belcher and I slap each other and begin laughing hysterically and then, like a gunshot—I hear my cue and Mary Ann Belcher yells, "Break a leg," and for good luck she kicks me in the knees with her steel-toed hiking boots and I stagger on stage, like this, and I confront Ebenezer Scrooge and I am the distilled embodiment of thespianism and I say, "Ebenezer Scrooge, I wear the chains I forged in life!" And the audience cheers and throws peanut butter and bitsy balls. And I triumphantly accept plaudits of the maddened crowd! And now you tell me, there's no *Christmas Carol?*

...

(Completely calm:) Cool. I'll get out these rags and go work out on the climbing wall for a couple of hours. *(Exiting:)* It would be nice if someone had told us because Mary Ann Belcher is back there weeping with her hands in the pickle juice.

> *(Marley is gone, slamming the door.)*

> *(Re-appearing:)*

And remember, there is nothing, nowhere, anywhere as dangerous as a disappointed thespian!

> *(Exits, slamming door. Immediately re-entering:)*

Nowhere.

> *(Marley exits, slamming door.)*

📖 **Discover** other comedies by Jon Jory with monologues, including *What Happens in Neverland Stays in Neverland, The Zoo Farce,* and *Identity Play.*

READ THE PLAY, a one-act holiday comedy for 15–48 actors:

yourstagepartners.com/the-semi-amazing-sort-of-sensational-almost-unbelievable-christmas-spectacular

What happens when a school tries to put on a Christmas Spectacular for the bargain price of $11.50? You get a ton of elves, a visit from the little match girl,  and a partridge in a pear tree. It may be low on budget, but it's high on laughs as we watch the Christmas characters we know and love hilariously collide in this Christmas disaster for the ages.

TOO MANY DETECTIVES AT THE MURDER MANSION
Ian McWethy

*There has been a murder in a mansion full of famous detectives, and the great Sherlock Holmes is being interrogated as a suspect by the less illustrious Detective Christie. However, when starstruck Christie asks Holmes to **prove** his famous powers of observation by deducing something about him, Holmes gives him more than he bargained for.*

SHERLOCK HOLMES

You're a mid-career detective. And given the state of your untucked shirt and the scuff marks on your shoes, I'd say you've given up any hope for advancement. Which you've been resigned to for some time now. I'd say ever since your thirty-fifth birthday. That was the day your brother-in-law, who makes a lot more money than you do, gave you that watch. It was meant as a gift, but whenever you look at it, it reminds you of the life you could have had. And of the status that you'll never achieve. It eats at you, haunts you, drags you down like an anchor every morning when you put it on. But for some reason, you cannot bear to *not* wear it. Because on some level, you feel like you deserve to be where you are.

…

…The main reason, I'd say, is that you're going through a contentious separation from your partner. One that has been going on for…six months now? No, seven!

…

The irritation around your ring finger suggests you've been taking your wedding ring off frequently. Furthermore, the circles under your eyes, the Cheeto dust under your fingernails! All the signs of a person who's been sleeping in an unfamiliar and sad bed. Likely a motel near the police station. It's there that you stay up late at night, eating your feelings in highly-processed food, asking yourself, "How did it all go so wrong? How is that I'm forty years old, living alone in a motel, watching re-runs of *Paw Patrol* until four in the morning? Why do I do it? Why?!"

✎ **Play** with the many faces of Holmes. From the original stories by Arthur Conan Doyle to the many adaptations and riffs on the character, Sherlock Holmes has appeared in many forms—but never quite like this. What can you bring from other depictions of Holmes to this character? What about this Holmes is unique? How can you have fun with a "serious" character in a comedic setting?

📖 **Discover** more plays by Ian McWethy with monologues, including *Last Day of School, I, Chorus, Win or Lose,* and *Mascots.*

READ THE PLAY, a full-length mystery-comedy for 10–20 actors:

yourstagepartners.com/too-many-detectives-at-the-murder-mansion-full-length

Sure, you think you've seen this type of murder mystery before. A cast of eccentric characters meet at a mansion, only to become suspects of a murder that a singular genius detective will eventually solve. But what happens when all the suspects are the detectives? Sherlock Holmes, Nancy Drew, Miss Marple, and Batman are just a few of the guests. *Too Many Detectives at the Murder Mansion* is a whodunnit that will leave you laughing and guessing right until the very end.

A one-act version of this play is also available.

THE SEVEN TORMENTS OF AMY AND CRAIG
adapted by Don Zolidis from his novel

*Seventeen-year-old Craig has messed up badly, and he knows it. He called his girlfriend Amy's decision to wait to have sex with him "unfair" because she's been with other guys before, and she promptly broke up with him. After he realizes how wrong he was to say this (with some help from his sister), Craig races to Amy's house at 2 a.m., ready to **grovel** like he has never groveled before—but more comes out than he may have intended.*

CRAIG

(In basically one breath:)

I am so sorry. I was an idiot. I don't know what's wrong with me. I probably wasn't raised right, and I never meant to get all jealous like that. That was so stupid, and I realize that I don't control your past and I can't judge you for anything you've done before, and there's like a horrible double standard thing and I don't even want to get into that right now, but it's okay, and of course it's okay. You've done things and that's completely fine—it's great actually, it's great, and I think the important thing is that I'm madly in love with you. And I know that you might not be in love with me, and I know that you are having a really hard time right now, in life, and I never, never want to make things harder on you. But I figure I don't want to hide my feelings towards you because you're the best thing that's ever happened to my life, even better than that time I went to Disney World. Way better than Disney World. Disney World actually kind of sucked because I threw up on Space Mountain and the puke got on these people behind me and they were screaming, and I thought they were going to kill me. So as soon as the ride was over, I ran away from the ride and got lost, and I ended up in the Hall of Presidents, which is basically horrible.

 Discover Don Zolidis comedies with monologues like *Haters* and *No Substitutes,* as well as his dramas that include monologues like *Monster* and *The Littlefield Gazette Does Not End Today.*

 Unlock monologues with obstacles: What obstacles are in your character's way to achieving their objectives? Are they physical obstacles? Mental obstacles? Is another character putting them there, or has the character set them up for himself?

What obstacles can you place in your character's way to physicalize their pursuit of an objective? As an exercise, imagine an objective across the room—and either come up with three obstacles to create a mini-obstacle course for your character to complete, or enlist a scene partner to surprise you by placing them in your path in the moment. A chair or closed door could be a simple, realistic obstacle, or they could stand for an imaginary snake or waterfall. What can you discover about how your character deals with obstacles in these moments as you speak your monologue?

READ THE PLAY, a full-length dramedy for 10–30 actors:

yourstagepartners.com/the-seven-torments-of-amy-and-craig-by-don-zolidis

In non-chronological order, Amy and Craig dissect and examine their tortuous first love affair in scenes that are both heartbreaking and hilarious. From their initial coupling on a second trip, to a series of increasingly awful disasters, this scabrously funny play tears apart the idea of true love…and maybe puts it back together again? Based on the bestselling YA novel.

REEL TIMES AT SOMERSET HIGH
TJ Young

Parker is a young movie obsessive who imagines everything in real life as a film genre—and moments after he meets a new student at school, Dallas, he is dismayed to **realize** *he's imagining a romance.*

PARKER

(In the manner of a soliloquy:)

Interior. My Locker. After lunch, but before gym class.

Oh my goodness. That was…new. Dallas. Oh what was life before Dallas? When will I see them again? I wonder if Dallas will be in gym class. I wonder if they ate something too heavy and the idea of running sprints across the gym floor will be too much for them. What a terrible first impression to have of how we do things here at Somerset. I think the first day at a new school should be easy. Simple. Relaxed. It's bad enough that you don't know anyone. Well, Dallas knows Ari. Kind of.

It's crazy to me that Ari didn't say anything else about Dallas. Like, what part of town they live in, how they were during the carpool…how cute they are.

Not that I noticed they are cute or anything like that. I barely saw them…from across the cafeteria right before an announcement about a stupid dance was made. I mean, I don't think it will be stupid per se. We do dances pretty well here. Homecoming last semester was a lot of fun. That's when Somerset really shows off, during our dances. I bet if Dallas went to the dance, they would really like this place.

Maybe…maybe I should ask Dallas. To the dance.

Why would they want to go with me? How would I even ask them?

What if they look at me and laugh because I look like someone from their old school, and they really disliked that person, because in fifth-period Chemistry they were lab partners and they never knew the difference between a solution and a solvent and a suspension! Although, I would need a refresher on that as well...

I cannot have a crush. There in no time for it. Between my presidential duties and not falling for people, my time is pretty well spent! Plus, am I the type of person who falls for that lame old cliche of love at first sight? How predictable would that be? Those are the WORST kinds of people. But, what if we did end up together and we became the type of people who carve our initials into a tree in the front of the school and come back some thirty years later when the flame has died to remind ourselves where it all began, kickstarting a renewed dedication to each other that can only be described as inspiration...that might not be so bad, actually. Noooooo. I can't have a crush. I've never had a crush before in my life. Unless you count Pat in the fourth grade, but I really just liked the fact that they had a classic Swamp Thing lunch box. The allure of that faded when I found out they hadn't even seen the seminal 1982 film. They didn't know who Wes Craven was! That wasn't a crush. That was a mistake in judgement.

(A bell rings.)

Ah! I'm late!

❧ **Note:** This role is listed as flexible, so Parker may be portrayed as a male character or not, as the actor or production desires. How will you build your character?

For this monologue, Parker's pronouns and the pronouns of any character mentioned may be modified as desired—all the roles in this play are flexible.

📖 **Discover** more of Parker's monologues in the full script of *Reel Times at Somerset High.* For more comedies by TJ Young, check out *The Inseparables* and *Isle of Noises.*

✐ **Play** with homage and references: Parker is a movie buff who puts himself into the cinema he loves. When the playwright writes "in the manner of the soliloquy," what media can you find that might be an inspiration for Parker's imagination in this moment? What characters might he connect with?

READ THE PLAY, a one-act comedy for 8–20+ actors:

yourstagepartners.com/reel-times-at-somerset-high

As President of the Film & TV Club, Parker prides themself on their knowledge of film and TV. They see the entire world as one big production: Math Class is a horror movie, the lunchroom is a cooking show, and Phys Ed is a war documentary. When a new student, Dallas, transfers to Somerset High, Parker discovers a new genre—romance. Soon a whole team of students with surprising talents are working together to help Parker make a big cinematic gesture in real life. But can you really connect with somebody you only see as a character? Maybe this isn't a rom-com—it's a joyfully hilarious coming-of-age story… with cow costumes.

Reel Times at Somerset High was developed through the Stage Partners One-Act Play Commission program with EdTA, and workshopped with a cast of Thespians from across the country at International Thespian Festival 2024, culminating in a premiere staged reading. 

101 BREAKUPS
Jason Pizzarello

*Trying to escape a terrible outdoor wedding, best man Jack and bridesmaid Jill have tumbled down a hill into what looks like an adorable burgeoning romance...until Jack panics and tries to **squash** it.*

JACK

We have to break up.

…

Sorry.

….

I know, we're not even together, but I see where this is going.

…

We just said we love each other, I know. It was beautiful. I meant it. I do. And I think we'll date very briefly before we get engaged. I don't have any doubt about that. And we won't wait long because we won't be able to. We'll have the most beautiful wedding. Not in this park. But near a waterfall. We'll barely be able to hear our vows over the rushing water. And we won't wait long either before having a little bird in the nest. A girl. And then another. A boy. And then another. A girl. And as we raise our three amazing children—oops we had one more—four. Our four amazing children we struggle and fight and make up and challenge ourselves again and again and fall more and more in love. Before we know it our children have children of their own. Except for that last one, he's in the peace corp. Anyway, life doesn't pass us by. We absorb it. And we grow old with grace and ease and still after all those years, are madly in love. And at the end of our lives we can't imagine it going any other way or ever being apart. The thought of being apart even in death, breaks me. I can't.

I can't handle the loss of you. The pain of losing you is worse than never having you in the first place. And so I think it's better if we just…don't.

Discover many more comedy plays by Jason Pizzarello, including *12 Angry Villains, Knock Knock, Two Chairs and A Lie, Parody This!,* and *This Murder Was Staged.*

Unlock monologues with music. As an exercise, try "scoring" your monologue as if your character were in a film. Play a piece of music underneath as you read it aloud to see what emotions, themes, or rhythms you can tease out in a surprising way. For example, in Jack's monologue from *101 Breakups,* how does it affect your performance if you accompany Jack's vision of future heartbreak with a sad song like Leonard Cohen's "Hallelujah"? Now, what happens if you score it with an ultra-dramatic piece of classical music, like Verdi's "Dies Irae"? How about Dolly Parton's "I Will Always Love You"? Experiment with songs with lyrics and instrumental music, each piece as different from the other as possible. The effect can be genuinely dramatic or incredibly goofy (especially for a comedy!). Remember, in a showcase performance or an audition, you won't really have a score—but by experimenting with music, you might discover a new way to approach a moment in your monologue that you can bring back to your performance.

READ THE PLAY, a one-act dramedy for 10–50 actors: yourstagepartners.com/101-breakups-by-jason-pizzarello

You'll feel all the feelings, but most especially, you'll feel hilariously moved in this dram-com that's bound to break your heart. 101 times.

WIN OR LOSE
Ian McWethy

*Here at the finish line of the absurd race he's concocted, the Coach has been defeated…or has he? His grand plan to make the senior class of Middleburg High competitive enough to be "winners" in the "real world" has been met with a rebellion, as all the students helped each other cross the finish line simultaneously. But maybe there's still a way to **motivate** this group…in a way…*

COACH

Okay, okay, okay! Everyone settle down! Settle!

(Everyone stops cheering. He glares at all of them.)

That was…by far…the saddest end to a competition I have ever seen in my life. My god. I'm disgusted. Your parents are considering disowning you! At the very least they are Googling "family law" to see what their options are!

(He looks at all of them.)

Well, I hope you're happy. I had but one dream when I started the Great Race of Middleburg High School. It was to teach you about the value of competition. To show you, all of you, what it feels like to strive for greatness. And for an elite few, why it matters to win. But today…well, you killed that dream for me. So congrats. You beat me. I lost.

*(And with that, Coach walks offstage solemnly.
Students cheer here!
But then he quickly turns around.)*

But if I lost. That means that you all, in fact, won. Which means the competition was really between me and all of you! Which means you all still competed in the Great Race, just a bigger one than you thought you were competing in! So remember that no matter what you do, as long as you live and breathe, there will always be a winner and loser!

Which means I still taught you a lesson. Which means that in some ways, I won too.

● **Meet** Coach: the playwright introduces Coach in a stage direction: "Athletic apparel. A whistle. Coach, in general, is always on. But today Coach is especially keyed up..."

● **Note:** This role is listed as flexible, so Coach may be portrayed as a male character or not, as the actor or production desires. How will you build your character?

READ THE PLAY, a one-act comedy for 10–20 actors:

yourstagepartners.com/win-or-lose

Competition is all that matters, and these kids today have got to learn that...by being pitted against each other in an absurdly grueling four-part race. Winner gets a scholarship. Come in last? You're banned from prom. The parents love it! But when different groupes at the beginning, middle, and end of the pack compare notes, commiserate and meet a local cautionary tale, they decide to play a different game altogether. An inventively staged, hilariously surreal winner of a one-act comedy. Because winning is all that matters in life, right? ...Right?!?

About the Authors

Visit www.yourstagepartners.com/authors to find each playwright's Stage Partners profile page. There you will find the playwright's full bio and links to each of their scripts in the Stage Partners catalogue. All scripts in the Stage Partners catalogue are available to read online in full.

ABOUT STAGE PARTNERS

Stage Partners is an independent play publisher dedicated to making exceptional plays accessible to all theatres and schools. Founded in 2015 by two playwrights with extensive backgrounds in theatrical publishing and licensing, Stage Partners was created with the simple idea that regardless of whether you are a new drama teacher or an experienced artistic director, finding the perfect new play should be easy, engaging, and exciting. With scripts that are always free to read, lightning-fast licensing, production & educational resources, and a passionate staff, Stage Partners is committed to offering industry-best services to both its customers and its playwrights. If you are looking for a publishing partner that understands that making theatre happen is hard work, but discovering a great new play should be a breeze, join us at www.yourstagepartners.com and we'll begin together.